WISER

TOGETHER

STUDY GUIDE

Books by Bill Hybels

The Power of a Whisper

Leadership Axioms

Holy Discontent

Just Walk Across the Room

The Volunteer Revolution

Courageous Leadership

Honest to God?

Fit to Be Tied (with Lynne Hybels)

Descending into Greatness (with Rob Wilkins)

Becoming a Contagious Christian
(with Mark Mittelberg and Lee Strobel)

Too Busy Not to Pray Study Guide (with Ashley Wiersma)

Life Lessons from Jesus (with John Ortberg)

The New Community Series
(with Kevin and Sherry Harney)

Colossians	*Philippians*	*The Sermon on the Mount 1*
James	*Romans*	
1 Peter		*The Sermon on the Mount 2*

The InterActions Small Group Series
(with Kevin and Sherry Harney)

Authenticity	*Jesus*	*New Identity*
Character	*Lessons on Love*	*Parenting*
Commitment	*Living in God's Power*	*Prayer*
Community		*Reaching Out*
Essential Christianity	*Love in Action*	*The Real Deal*
Fruit of the Spirit	*Marriage*	*Significance*
Getting a Grip	*Meeting God*	*Transformation*

WISER

TOGETHER

Learning
to Live the
Right Way

BILL HYBELS

with **SHANE FARMER** and **TODD KATTER**

ZONDERVAN

Wiser Together Study Guide
Copyright © 2012 by Willow Creek Community Church

This title is also available as a Zondervan ebook. Visit www.zondervan.com/ebooks.

Requests for information should be addressed to:

Zondervan, 3900 *Sparks Dr. SE, Grand Rapids, Michigan* 49546

ISBN 978-0-310-82010-9

Formatting and structure of this study were adapted from *40 Days in the Word: Work-book, Edition 1.0*, copyright © 2011 by Rick Warren.

Cover design: DogEared Design
Cover photography: iStockphoto®
Interior illustration: ShutterStock®
Interior design: Beth Shagene

Printed in the United States of America

14 15 16 17 18 19 /RRD/ 22 21 20 19 18 17 16 15 14 13 12 11 10 9 8 7 6 5 4 3 2 1

Contents

A Note from
Bill Hybels

Welcome to *Wiser Together*. A person who is wise is someone who has learned how to live life the right way. He or she is wise about relationships, wise about career, wise about money, wise about family, wise about character, and wise about eternity. "Wisdom is priceless!" says the writer of Proverbs.

All of us want to get better at life. Getting wiser *alone,* however, is just not the way it works. God didn't wire us to catch on to wise and godly living through lone-ranger attempts at learning; it's something that rubs off on us when we spend time with others who have the wisdom of God living inside them. As the proverb says, "Iron sharpens iron as one person sharpens another."

During the next five weeks, you are going to learn exactly how to spend time with others in a way that will help you grow, help you catch on to wisdom. And in return, you'll learn how to help *them* grow, and help *them* catch on to wisdom, as well.

Take these next five weeks seriously. Reflect on the proverbs daily. Memorize the verse of each week — and apply its wisdom to your life. Show up to your group consistently — and on time. Lean into developing your relationships with others in your group. Get to know them during group. Sit with them at church. Make time to be with them in the spaces between. And when at group, fully engage in the discussions.

Five weeks is going to fly by. If you make the *Wiser Together* experience a priority for just five weeks, I know God is going to show up. This is my hope for you.

Blessings,
Bill

A Guide
to Your Guide

Take a few moments to familiarize yourself with the features of this study guide:

Session Notes

Your Session Notes sections contain the questions that will be used as discussion guides during your five group gatherings. There also are fill-in-the-blank sections where you can take notes on Bill Hybels' teaching as you and your group watch the *Wiser Together* video.

Personal Journal

Set aside time during these next five weeks to read and reflect on the book of Proverbs. Your journal covers one chapter per day, six days a week, over the course of these five weeks. By the end of the five weeks, you will have read nearly the entire book of Proverbs. If reading and reflecting on Scripture is a fairly new practice for you, be sure to read below for tips on how to get the most out of your time in the Bible.

The Three Rs of Scripture

Engagement: Read

Read a section of Scripture. For this journal, you will be reading one chapter of Proverbs each day. Before you read, ask God to speak to you through his Word. Be sure to pay attention to what words or phrases really stand out to you.

Reflect

Once you've read the chapter, pick one verse for reflection. Perhaps a certain phrase or sentence stood out to you as you read. Choose the verse you have the most energy around and begin to reflect on it. Reflection is simply pondering what the phrase or sentence might mean.

Respond

If we simply read and reflect on God's truths without responding to him, we will never grow in wisdom. After reflecting, ask God how he wants you to respond. Simply ask him, "How do you want me to live differently because of this truth?" This helps us turn the truth we've reflected on into marching orders we can carry out in our lives. Maybe you need to start thinking differently or doing something differently. Is there something you need to stop doing or start doing because of this truth? Write down the exact way you are going to respond. Then do it!

Prayer

If you are looking for a framework to help you pray, try thinking of your prayer as having a C-H-A-T with God:

Confess

When we confess our sins, acknowledge Jesus as the One who died for our sins, and commit to turning away from sin and toward him, Scripture promises we will be forgiven. To confess any wrongs you have done to God, yourself, or others, start out by asking God to show you if you have sinned in any way. As something comes to mind, pray, "God, I confess I have sinned. I admit this was wrong. Jesus, I believe you died for my sins. Will you forgive me?"

Honor

Honoring God is simply another way of saying worshiping God. Take time simply to praise and honor God for who he is. Perhaps turn on worship music and listen to the words. Or write out worshipful words in your journal the way King David did in the Psalms. Honor God for his qualities, such as his goodness, love, and mercy.

Ask

The Bible clearly tells us God wants us to ask him for what we need. Make a list of the things you ask him for. Keep track of this list and continue to pray persistently until you get an answer. Jesus says that God loves to give good gifts to his children (Matthew 7:11). You might be surprised by how often he will say "yes" when you ask. Of course if he says "no," you can believe it's because he has your best interests at heart. Other times he will say "not yet," and you'll need to continue praying patiently but persistently.

Thank

End your prayer time by thanking God for anything you can think of to thank him for. Watch your heart grow in gratitude as you begin daily to thank God for his provision and realize his faithfulness in your life.

Small Group Resources

The appendices at the back of this workbook include materials that will help your group HOST prepare for your group. If you are a HOST, be sure to familiarize yourself with these resources.

WALKING WITH THE WISE

Gatherings that Grow

SESSION NOTES

Before You Gather

Whether your small group is brand new or an established gathering of old friends, you're starting something fresh with this study. You're going to connect with each other in a deeper way as we focus on how God designed us to become wiser *together*.

Warm-Up

Let's start by taking time to check in with one another.

QUESTION 1: Introduce yourself and describe the best experience of community you've ever had. Was it a small group, team, circle of friends, task force, or another community? Describe it in 60 seconds and share what made it unique.

QUESTION 2: Describe the worst group experience you've ever had. Was it a church small group, a committee, a group you had at work for an assignment, or a school group? What made it so bad?

VERSE OF THE WEEK

"Whoever walks with the wise becomes wise."
— PROVERBS 13:20 (ESV)

Video: Walking with the Wise

Watch the video teaching together. Use your study guide to take notes and fill in the blanks.

"You are who you hang around" was not just your mother's mantra. Jesus affirms the truth behind this saying in the gospel of Matthew: "For where two or three *gather* in my name, there am I with them" (Matthew 18:20, emphasis added). His prayer for his followers in the gospel of John states, "My prayer is not for them alone. I pray also for those who will believe in me through their message, that *all of them may be one*, Father, just as you are in me and I am in you" (John 17:20 – 21, emphasis added). And in Acts 2:44 – 47, the early church models what it looks like to walk together: "All the believers were together.... They broke bread in their homes and ate together with glad and sincere hearts, praising God and enjoying the favor of all the people."

The Scriptures are crystal clear that Christianity is intended to be a community in which no one _STANDS_ _ALONE_ .

The Goal

To become a gathering where everyone grows.

Definition of a failing small group: A gathering where, over time, nobody grows into Christlikeness.

Jesus' definition of growth (from Luke 10:27): "Love God with all your _HEART_ , _SOUL_ , _MIND_ , and _STRENGTH_ Love your _OTHERS_ as yourself."

Defining growth in loving God with all your:

Heart: Gatherings that grow provide a safe place for people to check in. **Soul:** Gatherings that grow stop to _PRAY_ for each other. **Mind:** Gatherings that grow discuss and apply

Scripture to their lives. **Strength:** Groups that grow leave with _PRACTICAL_ _STEPS_ _ACTIONS_ they plan to _DO_ .

Growth in Loving Others

1. Loving others well looks like _LISTENING_ .

2. Loving well means focusing more on others than on your own stories of accomplishment and experience.

3. Loving well in a group means confidentiality.

4. Loving well means the right balance of _GRACE_ and _TRUTH_ .

5. Loving well means keeping commitments and honoring others' time.

Discussion

READ TOGETHER: The word "discipleship" brings many things to mind. Some might picture one-to-one mentoring relationships. Others might picture a religious guru with a band of followers. However, discipleship actually means to grow as a follower of Christ's teachings. And helping others become his disciples is something all Christians are called to do.

In Matthew 28, Jesus gave his parting instructions, known as the "Great Commission," to his followers. He sent them on a _mission_ with clear marching orders: Make disciples. Go and help others learn how to put my teaching into practice in their lives.

Discipleship can take place in a variety of forms:

Relational: one-to-one

Presentational: one-to-many

Both of these are important to our mission to make disciples. Yet, we believe the best environment for the making of a disciple is within a group context.

Communal (group): many-to-many

QUESTION 3: Discuss how your participation in a small group could help others grow as disciples — to become wise instead of foolish. What are the benefits of the "many-to-many" community approach to discipleship?

QUESTION 4: The book of Proverbs has many admonitions against being shaped by the foolish ways of others. Describe a time when you did something foolish because of the influence of someone else.

QUESTION 5: In Matthew 28:19, Jesus tells his followers, "Go and make disciples of all nations." Have you ever thought of joining a small group as a way to live out the mission Jesus gave you to disciple others?

QUESTION 6: Jesus' words in Luke 10:27, often described as the "Greatest Commandment," tell his followers to "Love the Lord your God with all your heart and with all your soul and with all your strength and with all your mind." Which of these areas could use your focus right now?

- Does your **heart** need softening or healing?

- Does your **soul** need to experience more of God's Spirit?

- Do you need to utilize your **strength** to apply and live out what you already know?

- Does your **mind** need to learn and believe more of God's truth?

QUESTION 7: Are you in a season where you are seeking to invest relationally in others? Share with the group how you plan to grow in this area.

Deeper Study

Use the following questions if you have extra time, or if the group desires to dive in at greater length to this week's theme.

QUESTION 8: Read Hebrews 10:19 – 25 together. Notice there are three different commands that begin with the phrase, "let us." Each of these "let us" commands demonstrates how we are called to live because Jesus died and rose again for us. The third "let us" command specifically focuses on the importance of community. What aspects of community does it emphasize?

QUESTION 9: How does this passage of Scripture impact the priority that community should play in your life? In particular, how might you follow this "let us" command within the context of this group?

Closing

Review and sign the *Wiser Together* Group Agreement (see Appendix C).

PERSONAL JOURNAL

Set aside time each day to be intentional about your growth through the following exercises.

Day 1

READ: Proverbs 1

REFLECT: Matthew 18:20, *"For where two or three gather in my name, there am I with them."*

Why did Jesus emphasize coming together in this way?

RESPOND: What is Jesus asking you to do to apply today's reading to your life?

RECORD: Write your prayer.

Day 2

READ: Proverbs 2

REFLECT: Hebrews 10:24 – 25, *"And let us consider how we may spur one another on toward love and good deeds, not giving up meeting together, as some are in the habit of doing, but encouraging one another."*

Why do we underestimate the importance of spurring one another on toward love and good deeds?

Have you ever been encouraged in faith by a friend? Describe your encounter. Can you imagine that happening regularly? Can you imagine doing that for others regularly? How would these encouragements (both giving and receiving) impact your spiritual growth?

RESPOND: What is Jesus asking you to do to apply today's reading to your life?

RECORD: Write your prayer.

Day 3

READ: Proverbs 3

REFLECT: John 17:20 – 21, *"My prayer is not for them alone. I pray also for those who will believe in me through their message, that all of them may be one, Father, just as you are in me and I am in you."*

What does a group of people who are united look and feel like?

If you could imagine Jesus closing his eyes and picturing his church at this time, what do you think he pictures?

RESPOND: What can you do to make Christ's prayer for us as his church a reality? What is Jesus asking you to do to apply today's reading to your life?

RECORD: Write your prayer.

Day 4

READ: Proverbs 4

REFLECT: Acts 2:44 – 47, *"All the believers were together and had everything in common. They sold property and possessions to give to anyone who had need. Every day they continued to meet together in the temple courts. They broke bread in their homes and ate together with glad and sincere hearts, praising God and enjoying the favor of all the people. And the Lord added to their number daily those who were being saved."*

Which phrase or words stand out the most to you? Why?

Is the church simply a reflection of humanity's attempt to organize Christianity? Or is coming together essential to live out Christ's will? Explain your answer.

Which quality of the early church do you need to develop or strengthen in your life?

RESPOND: What is Jesus asking you to do to apply today's reading to your life?

RECORD: Write your prayer.

Day 5

READ: Proverbs 5

REFLECT: Luke 10:27, *"Love the Lord your God with all your heart and with all your soul and with all your strength and with all your mind; and love your neighbor as yourself."*

Which word or words really stand out to you in this verse? Why?

Read this verse, emphasizing one word at a time. (Example: LOVE God with …, love GOD with …, etc.) Do any new insights come to mind?

RESPOND: What is Jesus asking you to do to apply today's reading to your life?

RECORD: Write your prayer.

Day 6

READ: Proverbs 6

REFLECT: Matthew 28:18 – 20, *"Then Jesus came to them and said, 'All authority in heaven and on earth has been given to me. Therefore go and make disciples of all nations, baptizing them in the name of the Father and of the Son and of the Holy Spirit, and teaching them to obey everything I have commanded you. And surely I am with you always, to the very end of the age.'"*

This final commandment of Jesus, found at the end of Matthew's gospel, is often referred to as the "Great Commission." What parts of the Great Commission does Jesus instruct all his followers to join in?

How does this verse shape your view of becoming a disciple of Jesus?

RESPOND: What is Jesus asking you to do to apply today's reading to your life?

RECORD: Write your prayer.

THE COUNSEL OF COMMUNITY

Giving and Getting Wise Counsel

SESSION NOTES

Before You Gather

During your last gathering, you learned about God's plan for how we can become "wiser together." If there are new people at your gathering this week, you can look forward to learning from the unique wisdom they bring to your group. If you know their names, greet them; if you don't, introduce yourself.

Warm-Up

QUESTION 1: Do you have any wise mottos you try to live by? Maybe you have a phrase your parents said over and over, or perhaps you picked it up somewhere else, or even came up with it on your own. Share with the group one of your life mottos and why it has been an important reminder of wisdom for you.

QUESTION 2: How has the vision of how we become "wiser together" been evident in your life since we last met? Share an experience from this past week that brought this idea to mind. [Note: New people can take a pass on this question.]

> ### VERSE OF THE WEEK
>
> *"Where there is no guidance, a people falls, but in an abundance of counselors there is safety."*
>
> — PROVERBS 11:14 (ESV)

Video: The Counsel of Community

Watch the video teaching together. Use your study guide to take notes and fill in the blanks.

Wise counsel is one of the primary benefits to Christ followers of being fully engaged with a small group of believers. Today we are going to talk about what counsel should look like when we gather together.

The Right People

1. The right people for sharing wisdom are people who ___KNOW YOU___.

2. Christ's wisdom can be found everywhere in creation. However, we need to intentionally seek wisdom from those who ___KNOW___ and ___FOLLOW___ Christ.

   "The plans of the righteous are just, but the advice of the wicked is deceitful" (Proverbs 12:5).

3. The right people for receiving wisdom are ___WISE___ people.

Proverbs 9:7–9 says, "Whoever corrects a mocker invites insults; whoever rebukes the wicked incurs abuse. Do not rebuke mockers or they will hate you; rebuke the wise and they will love you. Instruct the wise and they will be wiser still; teach the righteous and they will add to their learning."

The purpose of a small group is to grow; therefore, when you are forming a group of believers to invest yourself in, seek out people for your inner circle who want to grow.

The Right Advice

Proverbs 27:9 says, "Perfume and incense bring joy to the heart, and the pleasantness of a friend springs from their heartfelt advice."

1. The right advice brings ___JOY___ to the heart.

2. The right advice is heartfelt advice.

3. The right advice comes from a ___FRIEND___ .

The DO NOTs of Counsel

1. Do not ___GIVE___ more counsel than you ___SEEK___ from others.

2. Never tell someone exactly what to do by giving commands, but instead offer advice that can be prayerfully considered.

3. Do not feel pressured to say something smart.

The DOs of Counsel

1. One of the most important things you can do when receiving counsel from others is to ___LISTEN___!

   Proverbs 25:12 says, "Like ... an ornament of fine gold is the rebuke of a wise judge to a listening ear." Remember: there is a kernel of truth in every critic.

2. Show your love for others before showing truth to them.

3. ___REBUKE___ in private; ___PRAISE___ in public.

4. Seek many counselors.

5. Discern when someone needs you to ___LISTEN___ versus when they really need ___ADVICE___ .

6. The best counsel comes in the form of questions.

7. Recommend a ___BOOK___ .

Discussion

QUESTION 3: Have someone read Proverbs 9:7 – 9 aloud (see the video notes). Without giving names, share a time when you gave counsel to someone and they were not open to it. In hindsight, why do you think they did not receive your counsel?

QUESTION 4: Counsel is often much easier to give than to receive. Share a time when someone gave you counsel and you didn't want to hear it. How would your life be different had you heeded their counsel? How did this affect your relationship with them?

QUESTION 5: Looking back on your life, is there a time when you wished you had asked for more counsel about how to grow in your relationship with God? What held you back?

QUESTION 6: Is there a time when you had another kind of need and wished you had asked for more counsel? Career? Emotional pain? Financial decisions? Large purchases? Relational or marital decisions? What might hold us back from getting solid counsel in these areas?

QUESTION 7: In Matthew 10:16 (ESV) Jesus says, "I am sending you out as sheep in the midst of wolves, so be wise as serpents and innocent as doves." With this in mind, Christians should not approach life with a naive sense that nothing can go wrong just because they are following Christ. What does it look like to maintain innocence while being wise?

Deeper Study

Use the following questions if you have extra time, or if the group desires to dive in at greater length to this week's theme.

Read Exodus 18 aloud. There are 24 verses in this chapter, so you may want to divide it up among a few of you.

QUESTION 8: From verses 9 – 12, what was Jethro's attitude when he came to meet Moses? Was he humble or prideful? Was he encouraging or critical?

QUESTION 9: Exodus 18:14 describes how, before offering advice, Jethro first asked two clarifying questions to get a better sense of the situation Moses was facing. How do you think this impacted Moses' willingness to listen to him (despite the fact that he was Moses' father-in-law)?

QUESTION 10: What lessons can you take from Jethro's approach to giving advice? When giving advice to others, what parts will you try to emulate? What parts will you change?

PERSONAL JOURNAL

Set aside time each day to be intentional about your growth through the following exercises.

Day 1

READ: Proverbs 7

REFLECT: Proverbs 12:5, *"The plans of the righteous are just, but the advice of the wicked is deceitful."*

What plans do you have today? This month? This year? Are your plans just? Have they been brought before a community of wise counselors who know Jesus?

What plans do you have in your career? Your family? Your faith? Your purchases? Are they just? Could you benefit from wise counsel?

RESPOND: What is Jesus asking you to do to apply today's reading to your life?

RECORD: Write your prayer.

Day 2

READ: Proverbs 8

REFLECT: Proverbs 9:7 – 9, *"Whoever corrects a mocker invites insults; whoever rebukes the wicked incurs abuse. Do not rebuke mockers or they will hate you; rebuke the wise and they will love you. Instruct the wise and they will be wiser still; teach the righteous and they will add to their learning."*

Have you ever gotten yourself into a bind by offering advice to the wrong person? Describe your situation, and what you learned.

Have you ever mocked or hated someone (v. 7) because they gave you advice? Why or why not?

Do you love those who rebuke you? Why or why not?

Do you appreciate instruction and teaching? Why or why not?

RESPOND: What is Jesus asking you to do to apply today's reading to your life?

RECORD: Write your prayer.

Day 3

READ: Proverbs 9

REFLECT: Proverbs 27:9, *"Perfume and incense bring joy to the heart, and the pleasantness of a friend springs from their heartfelt advice."*

Who in your life gives you heartfelt advice?

Do you have people in your life who are giving you non-heartfelt advice? What is the kernel of truth in their words?

To whom are you a friend? For whom do you have empathy and offer up heartfelt advice?

RESPOND: What is Jesus asking you to do to apply today's reading to your life?

RECORD: Write your prayer.

Day 4

READ: Proverbs 10

REFLECT: Proverbs 25:12, *"Like an earring of gold or an ornament of fine gold is the rebuke of a wise judge to a listening ear."*

Has there been a time when someone's words stung but helped you tremendously?

Are you a listening ear to those who are willing to speak harder truths to you?

How often do people share things with you that you would not necessarily like to hear? Why is that?

Would others consider you a wise person who appreciates counsel, guidance, advice, and truth?

RESPOND: What is Jesus asking you to do to apply today's reading to your life?

RECORD: Write your prayer.

Day 5

READ: Proverbs 11

REFLECT: Proverbs 27:5, *"Better is open rebuke than hidden love."*

Have you showed the people you love your appreciation for them lately?

In what ways are you hiding your love for others?

What is rebuke? Is it judgment? Is it condemnation? Is it redirection? What does Christlike rebuke look like?

RESPOND: What is Jesus asking you to do to apply today's reading to your life?

RECORD: Write your prayer.

Day 6

READ: Proverbs 12

REFLECT: Matthew 10:16 (ESV), in which Jesus says, *"I am sending you out as sheep in the midst of wolves, so be wise as serpents and innocent as doves."*

Are you increasingly wise like a serpent? Why or why not?

Do you have the innocence of a dove? Would others describe you that way? How can you be innocent and wise at the same time?

RESPOND: What is Jesus asking you to do to apply today's reading to your life?

RECORD: Write your prayer.

IRON
SHARPENS
IRON

How Groups
Make You Better

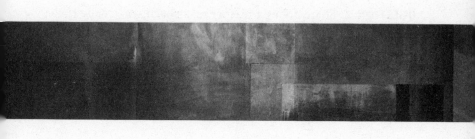

SESSION NOTES

Before You Gather

This is your third week together. For long-standing groups, this may be another in a series of many gatherings. But whether you are a new group or a group that's been gathering for years, every single time you meet, you are a new group — because new experiences have happened since you last met, some of which may have changed you forever. As you gather today, focus especially on how God may be using each of you to bring about positive change in the other members of the group.

Warm-Up

QUESTION 1: What is one way this series has impacted you so far?

QUESTION 2: Share about a teacher or a coach who really challenged you to grow in some way. What was it about them that made such an impact?

VERSE OF THE WEEK

"As iron sharpens iron, so one person sharpens another."
— PROVERBS 27:17

Video: Iron Sharpens Iron

Watch the video teaching together. Use your study guide to take notes and fill in the blanks.

Faith goes from _DULL_ to _SHARP_ in the context of community.

Is there a way in which we can come alongside each other and fundamentally help make each other better? How can we do that in a group context?

Four Pathways

Four primary pathways lead us toward transformation in the Christian life:

1. Knowing _TRUTH_

2. Experiencing God

3. Faith in _ACTION_

4. Relationships

Pathway 1—Knowing Truth

Faith-sharpening groups speak the truth to each other.

- We tell others the truth about _THEM_.
- We tell others the truth about _GOD_.

When speaking truth into another person, consider using a phrase like this: "I know you already know this. But it's good to remember … (fill in the truth here)."

Pathway 2—Experiencing God

1 John 4:12 says, "No one has ever seen God; but if we love one another, God lives in us and his love is made complete in us."

In being present with others, you help mediate God's _PRESENCE_ for others.

Pathway 3 — Faith in Action

Hearing others' examples of how they are applying their faith in everyday life is critical to helping you ___APPLY___ your faith.

Pathway 4 — Relationships

Consider the analogy of building a fire: If you separate the logs from one another, they each go out. But multiple logs, brought together, can burn brightly. This is true about Christianity; we don't burn brightly in secrecy and isolation. We don't burn brightly standing alone. We burn brightly when we are next to others who have the fire inside them as well.

Discussion

QUESTION 3: *Knowing Truth* — Share a truth about God that you need help remembering. Share a truth about yourself that you sometimes forget.

QUESTION 4: What's next? It's time to start thinking about what your group will do when you're finished with this five-week study. Discuss: Who wants to continue with the group for another study? Who might be interested in leading the next study?

QUESTION 5: *Experiencing God* — Marriage and family life expert Dr. Gary Chapman describes how humans receive love in his best-selling book, *The Five Love Languages.* Dr. Chapman proposes five unique "love languages":

- Words of affirmation
- Quality time
- Receiving gifts
- Acts of service
- Physical touch

Which of these love languages helps you feel most loved? Why?

QUESTION 6: Of the five love languages, which one did you receive most in your family of origin? Which one comes most naturally to you in expressing love to others? Why?

QUESTION 7: *Faith in Action* — Hearing testimonies of God's work in other people's lives can have a dramatic impact on our spiritual growth. Share an example of how hearing someone's story of faith (their testimony) has impacted your life.

QUESTION 8: *Relationships* — James 5:16 refers to the importance of relationships in helping us grow as disciples of Christ: "Therefore confess your sins to each other." How does confessing our sins to each other help us take steps on the path of spiritual transformation?

Deeper Study

Use the following questions if you have extra time, or if the group desires to dive in at greater length to this week's theme.

QUESTION 9: Hebrews 10:24 (ESV) encourages Christians to "consider how to stir up one another to love and good works." The image the author uses is one of a "stagnating" pot of stew that needs to be "stirred up" before it is served.

Determine which depiction better describes your small group: "stagnating" or "stirred up." On a scale of 1 to 10, how effective is your small group in "stirring up" each other to the life of love and good deeds to which God is calling you? What could you do in your group to help stir things up?

QUESTION 10: Read John 8:32 aloud. In a court of law, someone accused of a crime may be tempted to hide the truth. The truth, they fear, will be used against them. If everything they've done is discovered, they might be locked up and punished for it. However, when it comes to our spiritual lives, Jesus says in John 8:32 precisely the opposite: The truth won't get us locked up. No, Jesus says, the truth will break our chains of bondage. "The truth will set you free."

How could this viewpoint of truth change the ways we relate to each other as followers of Christ?

PERSONAL JOURNAL

Set aside time each day to be intentional about your growth through the following exercises.

Day 1

READ: Proverbs 13

REFLECT: 1 John 4:12, *"No one has ever seen God; but if we love one another, God lives in us and his love is made complete in us."*

Who do you encounter who is especially in need of receiving love? What are a couple of ways you can show God's love to someone today?

How do you need to receive God's love today? Is there anyone to whom you might reach out to express your need for love so they can be an encouragement to you?

RESPOND: What is Jesus asking you to do to apply today's reading to your life?

RECORD: Write your prayer.

Day 2

READ: Proverbs 14

REFLECT: James 5:16, *"Therefore confess your sins to each other and pray for each other so that you may be healed. The prayer of a righteous person is powerful and effective."*

Why do you think it is important to confess our sins to someone else?

Is there anything in your life you need to confess to someone today? To whom should you confess this?

How is God prompting you to grow in the biblical practice of confessing your sins regularly?

RESPOND: What is Jesus asking you to do to apply today's reading to your life?

RECORD: Write your prayer.

Day 3

READ: Proverbs 15

REFLECT: John 8:32, *"Then you will know the truth, and the truth will set you free."*

Who are the people in your life you can count on to tell you the truth?

Who is counting on you to tell the truth to them? Is there any truth you haven't spoken that you need to share?

What parts of your life currently feel like they are in bondage? How can you pursue truth in these areas so God can set you free?

RESPOND: What is Jesus asking you to do to apply today's reading to your life?

RECORD: Write your prayer.

Day 4

READ: Proverbs 16

REFLECT: John 14:6, *"Jesus answered, 'I am the way and the truth and the life. No one comes to the Father except through me.'"*

What does Jesus mean when he says he is the "truth"?

How can growing in your relationship with Jesus help you grow in understanding truth? What can you do today to learn more about who Jesus is?

With whom in your life today can you share the truth about Jesus?

RESPOND: What is Jesus asking you to do to apply today's reading to your life?

RECORD: Write your prayer.

Day 5

READ: Proverbs 17

REFLECT: James 3:13, *"Who is wise and understanding among you? Let them show it by their good life, by deeds done in the humility that comes from wisdom."*

How do your actions reflect the wisdom you have received from God? Have you done anything this past week that is contrary to what you know to be wise? If so, why?

How is it that the wiser we are, the more humble we are? Wouldn't you think it would be the opposite?

Is there anything you can do today to grow in humility?

RESPOND: What is Jesus asking you to do to apply today's reading to your life?

RECORD: Write your prayer.

Day 6

READ: Proverbs 18

REFLECT: Hebrews 5:13 – 14, *"Anyone who lives on milk, being still an infant, is not acquainted with the teaching about righteousness. But solid food is for the mature, who by constant use have trained themselves to distinguish good from evil."*

How would you assess your current maturity level in your relationship with Christ? Do you primarily feed on milk or solid food?

In what areas of your life do you feel like a beginner and need more "milk" to help you grow?

In what areas do you feel more mature and crave "solid food" to help you grow?

RESPOND: What is Jesus asking you to do to apply today's reading to your life?

RECORD: Write your prayer.

THE HEART OF COMMUNITY

Sharing Each Others' Joys and Sorrows

SESSION NOTES

Before You Gather

In this fourth week, we're learning about our hearts and the purpose of community. In today's gathering, pay special attention to how God might use you to be a blessing to another group member.

Warm-Up

QUESTION 1: Of the three previous *Wiser Together* sessions ("Walking with the Wise," "The Counsel of Community," and "Iron Sharpens Iron"), which one has had the greatest impact on your life? Why?

QUESTION 2: When was the last time you had your heart broken? Maybe it was a relationship that went south or a dream that didn't come true. Describe your broken-heart experience. Was there anyone who helped you navigate this difficult season?

VERSE OF THE WEEK

"Above all else, guard your heart, for everything you do flows from it."

— PROVERBS 4:23

Video: The Heart of Community

Watch the video teaching together. Use your study guide to take notes and fill in the blanks.

Biblical Descriptors of "Heart"

Pro 4:23

Sad	Angry	Scared	Happy	Excited	Tender
Sinking	Stubborn	Anxious	In love	Desiring	Responsive
Afflicted	Hardened	Troubled	Glad	Wanting	Broken
Despairing	Proud	Anguished	At peace	Committed	Contrite
Sick	Grudging	Distressed	Rejoicing	Devoted	
Weighed down	Hating	Failing	Cherishing	Yearning	
	Unyielding	Melting	Grateful	Craving	
	Callous	Afraid	Sincere		

Anything that is deep down ___INSIDE___ a person that we could not readily ___OBSERVE___ from watching them is considered to be "in their heart."

A summary of the Bible's use of the word "heart": The heart is the center of emotion, affection, and intention.

We can't apply outside-in solutions to inside-out problems.

MATT 6:21
PRO 3:5
~~*ROM 12:2*~~
PS 51:10
PS 34:18
MATT 15:18
LUKE 6:45

The Weekly Check-In

1. Share highs and lows.
2. Use great questions.

When Others Are Sharing

1. Refrain from ___SNAP___ ___JUDGMENTS___
2. ___LISTEN___ well.
3. Maintain ___EYE___ contact.

4. Express ___EMPATHY___.

"Rejoice with those who rejoice; mourn with those who mourn" (Romans 12:15).

5. Avoid ___INTERUPTING___ or ___UNECCASARY___ words.

6. No quick ___FIXES___ or easy ___ANSWERS___.

"Like one who takes away a garment on a cold day, or like vinegar poured on a wound, is one who sings songs to a heavy heart" (Proverbs 25:20).

Discussion

QUESTION 3: Practice what Bill just taught in this week's video. What was the highest point of your week? What was the lowest point?

QUESTION 4: Read Proverbs 25:20 aloud (see video notes). Describe a time when someone was trying to stay positive and cheerful around you, while you were going through something really tough. How did that feel? How did you hope they would respond?

QUESTION 5: Psychologists describe two components of listening well to someone, so they feel understood:

1. Affirm you understand the *content* of what they are saying.
2. Affirm your empathy for the *feelings* they are expressing.

When you were growing up, which aspect of listening — *content* or *feelings* — happened more naturally in your family of origin? Which aspect comes easier for you?

QUESTION 6: Romans 12:15 instructs us, "Rejoice with those who rejoice; mourn with those who mourn." What might this look like in the context of a small group? What barriers might keep you from doing this well?

QUESTION 7: Second Corinthians 12:10 says, "When I am weak, then I am strong." This verse reminds us that everything in spiritual community — this container for the heart — is the opposite of the world's order. Our weaknesses, not our areas of strength, are what move others; our sorrows, not our triumphs, break down barriers of shame and fear; our failures, not our successes, bind us together in hope. What areas of brokenness in your story could God use to help others as they share from their heart?

Deeper Study

Use the following questions if you have extra time, or if the group desires to dive in at greater length to this week's theme.

QUESTION 8: Psalm 23 (ESV) paints a beautiful picture of sheep being led by a good shepherd. "The Lord is my shepherd; I shall not want. He makes me lie down in green pastures. He leads me beside still waters. He restores my soul." This image of soul restoration depicts the safe community that Jesus the Good Shepherd longs for each of us to experience. On a scale of 1 to 10, share your perspective on the level of safety you feel in your small group. What can you do to increase your level of safety so that people feel comfortable sharing deeply from their heart?

QUESTION 9: Read Matthew 23:27 aloud. What metaphor does Jesus use to describe the Pharisees? Why do you think Jesus was so severe in his language?

QUESTION 10: From Matthew 23:27, how can you make sure that what Jesus said of the Pharisees isn't true of you? What part can your small group play in this?

PERSONAL JOURNAL

Set aside time each day to be intentional about your growth through the following exercises.

Day 1

READ: Proverbs 19

REFLECT: Proverbs 25:20, *"Like one who takes away a garment on a cold day, or like vinegar poured on a wound, is one who sings songs to a heavy heart."*

What is the state of your heart right now? Is it "light" or "heavy" or somewhere in between? How might this awareness impact the relationships you enter into today?

Do you know anyone who currently has a heavy heart? How can you show healthy support and comfort to them?

RESPOND: What is Jesus asking you to do to apply today's reading to your life?

RECORD: Write your prayer.

Day 2

READ: Proverbs 20

REFLECT: Romans 12:15, *"Rejoice with those who rejoice; mourn with those who mourn."*

What parts of your life cause you to rejoice? What parts cause you to mourn?

Do you know anyone rejoicing, with whom you can rejoice? Do you know anyone mourning, with whom you can mourn? How can you reach out to them today?

RESPOND: What is Jesus asking you to do to apply today's reading to your life?

RECORD: Write your prayer.

Day 3

READ: Proverbs 21

REFLECT: Galatians 6:2, *"Carry each other's burdens, and in this way you will fulfill the law of Christ."*

What burdens are you currently carrying? Whom do you know who will carry them with you?

Whom do you know who is carrying a significant burden? How can you reach out to them today to help carry their burdens?

RESPOND: What is Jesus asking you to do to apply today's reading to your life?

RECORD: Write your prayer.

Day 4

READ: Proverbs 22

REFLECT: 2 Corinthians 12:9 – 10, *"But [the Lord] said to me, 'My grace is sufficient for you, for my power is made perfect in weakness.' Therefore I will boast all the more gladly about my weaknesses, so* *that Christ's power may rest on me. That is why, for Christ's sake, I delight in weaknesses, in insults, in hardships, in persecutions, in difficulties. For when I am weak, then I am strong."*

Where do you feel weak today? What might it look like for you to boast in your weakness today?

In what way can your weakness actually be a strength? How does your weakness help you see your desperate need for Christ?

How can you encourage someone else through the areas where you feel weak?

RESPOND: What is Jesus asking you to do to apply today's reading to your life?

RECORD: Write your prayer.

Day 5

READ: Proverbs 23

REFLECT: Matthew 23:27, *"Woe to you, teachers of the law and Pharisees, you hypocrites! You are like whitewashed tombs, which look beautiful on the outside but on the inside are full of the bones of the dead and everything unclean."*

What parts of your life feel particularly dark today? In what ways are you tempted to hide the dark parts inside of you?

How can you express to others some of the darker parts of your life? What ingredients are required in those relationships for you to do this in a safe way?

RESPOND: What is Jesus asking you to do to apply today's reading to your life?

RECORD: Write your prayer.

Day 6

READ: Proverbs 24

REFLECT: Psalm 23:1 – 3a, *"The LORD is my shepherd, I lack nothing. He makes me lie down in green pastures, he leads me beside quiet waters, he refreshes my soul."*

Where do you need God to shepherd you today? What guidance do you desperately need?

How can you find green pastures and quiet waters in the midst of your day?

What would it look like for your soul to be completely refreshed? How can you pursue that today?

RESPOND: What is Jesus asking you to do to apply today's reading to your life?

RECORD: Write your prayer.

FAITH AND FRIENDSHIP

How Small Groups and Friendships Work Together

SESSION NOTES

Before You Gather

This final week of our *Wiser Together* study explores how close relationships impact every part of our lives. In this group session, pay attention to how God may be using the relationships in your group to help each person grow *after* this study ends.

Warm-Up

QUESTION 1: In the last official week of our *Wiser Together* study, let's take a few minutes to share highlights. Describe how this study has changed your thinking about what it takes to become "wiser together." What is the most impactful takeaway for you?

QUESTION 2: Last week, we talked about how to check in with each other weekly by sharing a high point and low point since the last time we met. What is your "high/low" for the week?

QUESTION 3: In this session, we're talking about the importance of friendship. Who was your best friend growing up? What made this person your best friend? What fun things did you enjoy doing together?

Video: Faith and Friendship

Watch the video teaching together. Use your study guide to take notes and fill in the blanks.

The Space Between

1. Go beyond __EXPECTED__ during times of __ADVERSITY__.

   "A friend loves at all times, and a brother is born for a time of adversity" (Proverbs 17:17).

   Going beyond what is expected requires you to take initiative and go out of your way to do something that was not asked for.

2. Do your __NORMAL__ __ROUTINE__ together.

3. Give it __TIME__ to grow.

   Keep in mind that all friends fight.

   Conflict is often the gateway to deeper community if you stick it out and work toward resolution.

4. __BE__ a friend before you __SEEK__ a friend.

Committing to Community

1. Commit to being in a small group.

2. Commit to regular time in prayer and Bible study.

3. Commit to your own pursuit of community, and to helping others get connected as well.

Discussion

QUESTION 4: Read Proverbs 17:17 (see video notes). Have you ever had a friend support you through a difficult time? If so, describe your experience. If you were looking for support and didn't get it, how did you feel?

QUESTION 5: Research[1] shows the time we invest in friendships dramatically declines from adolescence to adulthood. As teenagers, we spend nearly a third of our time with friends. For the rest of our lives, we spend less than a tenth of our time with our friends. Why do you think that is? Has this been true in your life?

QUESTION 6: Bill closed this session with three commitments (see video notes). What are your thoughts about each of these commitments? If the group will be continuing on with another study, choose a date and a study for the first gathering, even if holidays or trips mean you won't begin meeting again for a few weeks.

---

1. Tom Rath, *Vital Friends: The People You Can't Afford to Live Without* (New York: Gallup Press, 2006).

QUESTION 7: How full is your friendship bucket? Which relationship season describes you?

- Looking for friends
- Content with the level of friendships I currently have
- Not able to keep up with the number of friends I have

QUESTION 8: Have you ever felt like you were on the "outside" of a clique of friends? What did it feel like? How has this experience impacted your behavior when you've been an "insider" in a group?

QUESTION 9: What next steps do you feel God might want you to take in pursuing deeper friendships in your life? How can this group help you?

Deeper Study

Use the following questions if you have extra time, or if the group desires to dive in at greater length to this week's theme.

QUESTION 10: Read John 15:12–17 aloud. In the Jewish culture of Jesus' day, the students of a rabbi were seen as his servants and so naturally kept a relational distance from him. Thus, Jesus completely shocked his disciples when he told them in John 15:15 they were no longer his *servants*, but his *friends*. But Jesus didn't mean that his disciples could do as they pleased; the requirement for "friendship with God" is obedience to his commands. What does it mean to be a "friend" of God? How might this influence your desire and attitude as you seek to obey him?

QUESTION 11: In John 15, Jesus called his disciples to love one another, even to the point of laying down their lives for each other if needed (v. 13). He painted a radical vision of friendship and sacrifice for the community of his followers. What does it mean to pursue radical friendship in our day? Is friendship optional? Is it possible to be a fully devoted follower of Christ and not have any close friends?

QUESTION 12: Jesus told his disciples that he chose them (John 15:16) and called them his friends (v. 14). Does Jesus call us to the ministry of friendship today? What does it look like to pursue friendship with others as a calling from God?

PERSONAL JOURNAL

Set aside time each day to be intentional about your growth through the following exercises.

Day 1

READ: Proverbs 25

REFLECT: Proverbs 25:17, *"Seldom set foot in your neighbor's house — too much of you, and they will hate you."*

Which friends are you most likely to spend too much time with? Too little time?

Is there anyone who spends more time with you than you'd like, and by whom you feel a bit smothered? How can you be loving toward them while also creating healthier boundaries?

RESPOND: What is Jesus asking you to do to apply today's reading to your life?

RECORD: Write your prayer.

Day 2

READ: Proverbs 26

REFLECT: Matthew 4:18 – 19, *"As Jesus was walking beside the Sea of Galilee, he saw two brothers, Simon called Peter and his brother Andrew. They were casting a net into the lake, for they were fishermen. 'Come, follow me,' Jesus said, 'and I will send you out to fish for people.'"*

Why was Jesus so intentional in selecting the disciples, his closest group of friends?

In thinking about your closest friends, how did you become friends? How intentional have you been in deepening each friendship?

How can you invest in your friendships for the purpose of growing spiritually? Are there any new friendships you sense you should seek out?

RESPOND: What is Jesus asking you to do to apply today's reading to your life?

RECORD: Write your prayer.

Day 3

READ: Proverbs 27

REFLECT: Proverbs 27:10a, *"Do not forsake your friend or a friend of your family."*

When was the last time you felt forsaken by a friend or a family member? Is there any amount of forgiveness you still need to give them?

Which friend or family member needs your help right now? What can you do today to support them?

RESPOND: What is Jesus asking you to do to apply today's reading to your life?

RECORD: Write your prayer.

Day 4

READ: Proverbs 28

REFLECT: John 15:15, *"I no longer call you servants, because a servant does not know his master's business. Instead, I have called you friends, for everything that I learned from my Father I have made known to you."*

What does it mean to be a friend of Jesus? In what ways does your relationship with him reflect a true friendship?

As a friend of Jesus, who might he want you to reach out to and befriend today?

RESPOND: What is Jesus asking you to do to apply today's reading to your life?

RECORD: Write your prayer.

Day 5

READ: Proverbs 29

REFLECT: John 15:13, *"Greater love has no one than this: to lay down one's life for one's friends."*

Who are your closest friends? Would you risk your own life for theirs? Which of your friends would lay down their life for you?

How does sacrifice play into building friendships? What sacrifice could you make to show care and support for a friend who is in a difficult spot right now?

RESPOND: What is Jesus asking you to do to apply today's reading to your life?

RECORD: Write your prayer.

Day 6

READ: Proverbs 30

REFLECT: Romans 12:10 (ESV), *"Love one another with brotherly affection. Outdo one another in showing honor."*

What does it look like to love someone with brotherly affection? With which of your friends does this come naturally?

How do you show honor to your friends? What particular action can you take today to show honor to a friend who may be in need of it?

RESPOND: What is Jesus asking you to do to apply today's reading to your life?

RECORD: Write your prayer.

SMALL GROUP RESOURCES

FAQs for the HOST

Find answers to frequently asked questions about being a small group HOST.

What is a HOST?

A HOST is the person who coordinates and facilitates your group meetings. The HOST may lead the group discussions themselves, or may take turns doing so with one or more group members. Several other group-leading responsibilities can be rotated as well, including supplying refreshments, gathering the group's prayer requests, or keeping up with those who miss a meeting. Shared ownership in the group helps everyone grow.

The four prerequisites for being a HOST are simple:

Heart for people

Open a space

Share a snack

Turn on the video

How much of my time will this take?

The group will gather for two hours every week. Of course, if you decide to share a meal together, this could extend your time.

Outside of group time, you'll simply need to look over the session notes in your study guide ahead of time. This should take no more than twenty or thirty minutes.

Where do I find new group members?

If you're new to the area or new to the church, this can be especially challenging. Be sure to read Appendix D, "Inviting Others into Your Group," for ideas on how to brainstorm a list of potential group members from your workplace, church, school, neighborhood, family, and so on. Also, utilize any opportunities your church provides to connect with others and form new relationships. And remember, your group doesn't need to be large. Even finding two other people you can gather with for these sessions is enough for an impactful group experience.

What do we do with our children during meetings?

If someone in your group has children old enough to supervise little ones, perhaps designate one room in the house where the older kids will hang out with or babysit the younger ones. Or consider having those with children chip in to hire a babysitter who can care for the kids in a separate room of the house or in a home nearby.

Will there be homework? If so, how much?

Beyond the journal pages that all group members are encouraged to use, there is no homework during the week. Be sure to look over the week's session ahead of time, and take a few moments to pray in preparation for your gathering. This should take you less than a half hour per week.

Do I have to talk or can I just sit and listen during meetings?

You, or someone else in the group, will need to facilitate the conversation. This requires making sure each question gets read aloud so the group can respond, and encouraging others to participate if no one is talking.

Do I have to pray aloud?

No. If you're not comfortable praying aloud, you may simply ask if someone in the group would be comfortable starting and ending the group by praying aloud.

Who else will be in the group?

This group is designed to be built by you, from the people you already know and have connections with. Invite friends, family, neighbors, colleagues, and of course those you've met at church.

How much do I have to know about the Bible?

You don't have to know anything about the Bible. You won't be required to give answers.

How many weeks will this group last?

Five weeks. Your group might choose to add a sixth week as a celebration, but this is optional. Also, in your final week, each group member may decide if he or she desires to continue together with another study.

If I don't like it, can I leave without people being angry with me?

As the HOST, you're asked to commit to sticking it out for the five-week run. At the end of that time, you have no obligation to continue hosting or participating in the group.

What will we do during meetings?

Your group will follow the session order for each week as laid out in this *Wiser Together* study guide. This will involve watching the week's video together and discussing the corresponding questions in the guide.

Top Ten Tips
for the HOST

Congratulations! As the HOST of your small group, you have responded to the call to help gather the church for the sake of growth. Few other tasks in the family of God surpass the kingdom contribution you will be making. As you prepare to facilitate your group, whether for one week or the entire series, here are a few thoughts to keep in mind.

Remember you are not alone. God knows everything about you, and he knew you would be facilitating your group. You may not feel ready, but God promises, "I will never leave you; I will never abandon you" (Hebrews 13:5 GNB). Whether you are facilitating for one evening, several weeks, or longer, you will be blessed as you serve.

1. **Don't try to do it alone.** Pray for God to help you build a healthy team. If you can enlist a cohost to help you prepare for and guide the group experience, go for it. This is your chance to involve as many people as you can in building a healthy group. All you have to do is ask people to help. You'll be surprised at the response.

2. **Be friendly and be yourself.** God wants to use your unique gifts and temperament. Greeting people warmly at the door can set the mood for the whole gathering. Remember, some people may feel they are taking as big a step to show up at your place as you are to host a small group. Don't try to do things exactly like another HOST; do them in a way that fits you. Admit when you don't have an answer and apologize when you make a mistake. Be authentic. Your group will love you for it and you'll sleep better at night.

3. **Prepare for your meeting ahead of time.** Review the session and write down your responses to each question.

4. **Pray for your group members by name.** Before your group arrives, take a few moments to pray for each member by name. You may want to review the Prayer Tracker (Appendix E) each week as you do this. Ask God to use your time together to touch the heart of each person

in your group. Expect God to lead you to whomever he wants you to encourage or challenge in a special way. If you listen, God will surely lead.

5. **When you ask a question, be patient.** Someone will eventually respond. Sometimes people need a moment or two of silence to think about the question. Don't react too quickly to a bit of silence. If silence doesn't bother you, it won't bother anyone else. After someone responds, affirm the response with a simple "thanks" or "great answer." Then ask, "How about somebody else?" or "Would someone who hasn't shared like to add anything?" Be sensitive to new people or reluctant members who aren't ready to speak, pray, or do anything. If you give them a safe setting, over time they will become more comfortable. If someone in your group is a wallflower who sits silently through every session, consider talking with them privately and encouraging them to participate. Assure them that they offer valuable insights, which will be greatly appreciated.

6. **Encourage group participation with each question.** Ask if anyone would like to read the paragraph or Bible passage. Don't call on anyone, but ask for a volunteer, and then be patient until someone begins. Be sure to thank the person who reads aloud.

7. **Break into smaller groups occasionally.** Sharing in a smaller circle can improve the whole experience. If your group is large, consider doing part of the discussion time in smaller circles, then reconvene near the end.

8. **Rotate facilitators occasionally.** You may be perfectly capable of hosting each time, but you will help others grow in their faith and gifts if you give them opportunities to facilitate the group.

9. **Try to discern what's next.** For some groups, the five-week session will be a great short-term engagement that will grow some friendships and equip them for the days ahead — but they may not ever meet again as a group. They committed to five weeks and should not be pressured to do anything beyond that. However, keep a prayerful heart about what God might be up to. Is he doing something in your group that should continue past the five weeks? Is there someone else in the group who might be the right person to lead the group into the future after these five weeks are over? What will your long-term role be in the future? Will you continue to utilize your space to host? Will

you become the group's leader in the future? Ask God to show you what's next and ask the group to do the same.

10. **Prepare your heart.** Reflect on the Bible passages that follow as a way of preparing your heart ahead of time — perhaps one per day for the next six days. If you'll do this, you'll be more than ready for your first meeting.

> When he saw the crowds, he had compassion on them, because they were harassed and helpless, like sheep without a shepherd. Then he said to his disciples, "The harvest is plentiful but the workers are few. Ask the Lord of the harvest, therefore, to send out workers into his harvest field."
>
> — MATTHEW 9:36 – 38

> I am the good shepherd; I know my sheep and my sheep know me — just as the Father knows me and I know the Father — and I lay down my life for the sheep.
>
> — JOHN 10:14 – 15

> Be shepherds of God's flock that is under your care, watching over them — not because you must, but because you are willing, as God wants you to be; not pursuing dishonest gain, but eager to serve; not lording it over those entrusted to you, but being examples to the flock. And when the Chief Shepherd appears, you will receive the crown of glory that will never fade away.
>
> — 1 PETER 5:2 – 4

> Therefore if you have any encouragement from being united with Christ, if any comfort from his love, if any common sharing in the Spirit, if any tenderness and compassion, then make my joy complete by being like-minded, having the same love, being one in spirit and of one mind. Do nothing out of selfish ambition or vain conceit. Rather, in humility value others above yourselves, not looking to your own interests but each of you to the interests of the others. In your relationships with one another, have the same mindset as Christ Jesus.
>
> — PHILIPPIANS 2:1 – 5

> Let us hold unswervingly to the hope we profess, for he who promised is faithful. And let us consider how we may spur one another on toward love and good deeds, not giving up meeting

together, as some are in the habit of doing, but encouraging one another — and all the more as you see the Day approaching.

— HEBREWS 10:23 – 25

Instead, we were like young children among you. Just as a nursing mother cares for her children, so we cared for you. Because we loved you so much, we were delighted to share with you not only the gospel of God but our lives as well.... For you know that we dealt with each of you as a father deals with his own children, encouraging, comforting and urging you to live lives worthy of God, who calls you into his kingdom and glory.

— 1 THESSALONIANS 2:7 – 8, 11 – 12

WISER TOGETHER Group Agreement

During our five weeks together, we will focus on helping each other grow in holistic love of God and love of others.

Love God

HEART: We provide space at our gathering for everyone to check in at a heart level. We make this depth of sharing safe by listening well and avoiding thoughtless answers, snap judgments, or quick fixes.

SOUL: We never leave our gathering without having someone pray on behalf of the group and ask God to meet our needs.

MIND: We engage in biblical teaching by watching the video together and engaging in discussion.

STRENGTH: We strive to put what we learn each week into practice in our lives. We give others permission to speak wisdom lovingly into our lives that could help us grow.

Love Others

- We commit to listening more than we talk.
- We commit to keeping confidential everything shared in this group. We balance grace with truth.
- We keep commitments we make with the group.
- We honor one another's time by showing up on time and by contacting the group HOST if we cannot attend.
- We focus more on others than on representing our own stories of accomplishment and experience.
- We avoid gossip, handling any conflicts by following Jesus' guidelines for conflict resolution as found in Matthew 18:15 – 17.

I commit to upholding the values stated in this agreement.

SIGNATURE _____   DATE _____

Inviting Others into Your Group

Utilize this brainstorming exercise and process to help you expand your group.

Brainstorm your circle of life:

1. **List** one or two people in each circle.
2. Prayerfully **select** one person or couple from your list and talk with your group about the possibility of inviting them.
3. **Invite** them to your next meeting. More than 50 percent of those invited to a small group say, "Yes!"

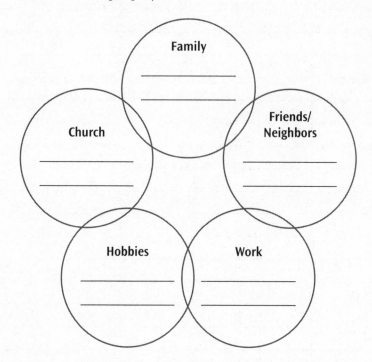

(Adapted from Saddleback Church. Used with permission.)

Prayer Tracker

Record the prayer requests from members of your group and keep track of answered prayers. If you are unsure how to pray, consider using a sentence like this to get you started:

"God, please help _____ to _____."

Date	Person	Prayer Request	Report
8/10/14	Joe	friend to get job	

Answer Key

Missing some of the answers to one of the video sessions? Find answers here.

Session 1: Walk with the Wise

The Scriptures are crystal clear that Christianity is intended to be a community in which no one **stands alone**.

The Goal

Jesus' definition of growth (from Luke 10:27):

"Love God with all your **heart**, **soul**, **strength**, and **mind**. Love your **neighbor** as yourself."

Defining growth in loving God with all your ...

Soul: Gatherings that grow stop to **pray** for each other.

Strength: Groups that grow leave with **practical actions** they plan to **do**.

Growth in Loving Others

1. Loving others well looks like **listening**.

4. Loving well means the right balance of **grace** and **truth**.

Session 2: The Counsel of Community

The Right People

1. The right people for sharing wisdom are people who **know you**.

2. Christ's wisdom can be found everywhere in creation. However, we need to intentionally seek wisdom from those who **know** and **follow** Christ.

3. The right people for receiving wisdom are **wise** people.

The Right Advice

1. The right advice brings **joy** to the heart.

3. The right advice comes from a **friend**.

The DO NOTs of Counsel

1. Do not **give** more counsel than you **seek** from others.

The DOs of Counsel

1. One of the most important things you can do when receiving counsel from others is to **listen**!
3. **Rebuke** in private; **praise** in public.
5. Discern when someone needs you to **listen** versus when they really need **advice**.
7. Recommend a **book**.

Session 3: Iron Sharpens Iron

Faith goes from **dull** to **sharp** in the context of community.

Four Pathways

Four primary pathways lead us toward transformation in the Christian life:

1. Knowing **truth**
3. Faith in **action**

Pathway 1 — Knowing Truth

- We tell others the truth about **them**.
- We tell others the truth about **God**.

Pathway 2 — Experiencing God

In being present with others, you help mediate God's **presence** for others.

Pathway 3 — Faith in Action

Hearing others' examples of how they are applying their faith in everyday life is critical to helping you **apply** your faith.

Session 4: The Heart of Community

Anything that is deep down **inside** a person that we could not readily **observe** from watching them is considered to be "in their heart."

When Others Are Sharing

1. Refrain from **snap judgments**.
2. **Listen** well.

3. Maintain **eye** contact.

4. Express **empathy**.

5. Avoid **interrupting** or **unnecessary** words.

6. No quick **fixes** or easy **answers**.

Session 5: Faith and Friendship
The Space Between

1. Go beyond **expected** during times of **adversity**.

2. Do your **normal routine** together.

3. Give it **time** to grow.

4. **Be** a friend before you **seek** a friend.

Group Roster

It's important for the people in your group to have each other's contact information so you can connect with each other between meetings. Collect each person's information below, and be sure to add any other details that might help you stay in touch.

Name	Email	Preferred Phone	Other (second phone/Facebook/etc.)

Group Calendar

Healthy groups share responsibilities and ownership for the group. It might take some time for this to develop. Shared ownership ensures that responsibility for the group doesn't fall to one person. Use the calendar that follows to keep track of group meetings, social events, serving projects, etc. Complete this calendar during your first or second meeting. Planning ahead ensures people can attend and helps more people get involved. (See next page.)

Group Calendar

Meeting	Date/Time	HOST	Location	Person(s) Providing Snack/Meal
Session 1				
Session 2				
Session 3				
Session 4				
Session 5				
Celebration (optional)				
Service Day (optional)				
Other				

Memory Verses

Commit one verse of Scripture to memory each week.

Session 1: Walking with the Wise

"Whoever walks with the wise becomes wise."
— PROVERBS 13:20 (ESV)

Session 2: The Counsel of Community

"Where there is no guidance, a people falls, but in an abundance of counselors there is safety."
— PROVERBS 11:14 (ESV)

Session 3: Iron Sharpens Iron

"As iron sharpens iron, so one person sharpens another."
— PROVERBS 27:17 (NIV)

Session 4: The Heart of Community

"Above all else, guard your heart, for everything you do flows from it."
— PROVERBS 4:23 (NIV)

Session 5: Faith and Friendship

"A man of many acquaintances may come to ruin, but there is a friend who sticks closer than a brother."
— PROVERBS 18:24 (PARAPHRASED)

Too Busy Not to Pray
DVD Study
Slowing Down to Be with God

Bill Hybels with Ashley Wiersma

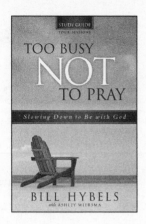

Bestselling author and pastor Bill Hybels offers timeless concepts based on his book of the same name that has sold over one million copies, helping individuals and small groups develop an understanding and enjoyment of prayer.

The urgent need for prayer in today's broken world is clear, but busyness still keeps many of us from finding time to pray. So Bill Hybels offers us his practical, time-tested ideas on praying effectively.

In this four-session video Bible study based on his classic book on prayer, *Too Busy Not to Pray*, Bill Hybels calls us to make prayer a priority, broadening the vision for what our eternal, powerful God does when his people slow down to pray.

The coordinating study guide (sold separately) leads individuals and small groups through discussion topics, group activities, and in-between-studies assignments.

The session titles include:

1. Why Pray?
2. Our Part of the Deal
3. When Prayer Feels Hard
4. People of Prayer

Hybels helps you listen to God and learn how to respond. As a result, you will grow closer to God and experience the benefits of spending time with him.

Available in stores and online!

The Power of a Whisper DVD Curriculum

Hearing God.
Having the Guts to Respond.

Bill Hybels

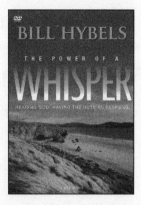

God still speaks — is anyone listening? Join bestselling author and pastor Bill Hybels in this four-session video-based study where your group will learn to navigate life through whispers from God. Through this dynamic teaching and group study, you will learn to practice hearing from God, surrender to the voice of God, obey his promptings and become a more effective kingdom-builder. Use with the *Power of a Whisper Participant's Guide* to help facilitate group discussion and further study.

Available in stores and online!

Just Walk Across the Room

DVD Curriculum

Four Sessions on Simple Steps Pointing People to Faith

Bill Hybels with Ashley Wiersma

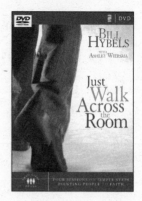

In *Just Walk Across the Room*, Bill Hybels brings personal evangelism into the twenty-first century with a natural and empowering approach modeled after Jesus himself. When Christ "walked" clear across the cosmos more than two thousand years ago, he had no forced formulas and no memorized script; rather, he came armed only with an offer of redemption for people like us, many of whom were neck-deep in pain of their own making.

This dynamic four-week experience is designed to equip and inspire your entire church to participate in that same pattern of grace-giving by taking simple walks across rooms—leaving your circles of comfort and extending hands of care, compassion, and inclusiveness to people who might need a touch of God's love today.

This DVD is designed for use in conjunction with *Just Walk Across the Room: The Four-Week Campaign Experience*, which consists of three integrated components:

- Sermons, an implementation guide, and church promotional materials provided on CD-ROM to address the church as a whole
- Small group DVD and a participant's guide to enable people to work through the material in small, connected circles of community
- The book *Just Walk Across the Room* to allow participants to think through the concepts individually

Available in stores and online!